Cows, Crops and a Pony

Allan E. Lange

iUniverse, Inc.
New York   Bloomington

Cows, Crops and a Pony

Front Cover Photo: August Lange Sr. and Grandson Allan E. Lange, 1940's

iUniverse books may be ordered through booksellers or by contacting:

iUniverse
1663 Liberty Drive
Bloomington, IN 47403
www.iuniverse.com
1-800-Authors (1-800-288-4677)

Because of the dynamic nature of the Internet, any Web addresses or links contained in this book may have changed since publication and may no longer be valid.

ISBN: 978-1-4502-2954-8 (sc)
ISBN: 978-1-4502-2955-5 (ebk)

Library of Congress Control Number: 2010906299

Printed in the United States of America

iUniverse rev. date: 5/13/2010

Dedicated to my wife Patricia
Thanks for the inspiration and
all the endless hours of hard work

THE LANGE FARM
TAKEN IN 1940's

The written story of a life give insight of the times that the individual experiences and how it shapes that life. It points out the environment that existed and tells of people that influenced that person.

INTRODUCTION

I was born the same day that my grandmother was buried. It was a cold morning on February 2, 1934, Ground Hog Day. My father didn't know whether to be happy or sad. I was the youngest of four children. My brother Gerald was nineteen, older sister, Doris was fifteen and my other sister Phyllis was six. I was born in our farm house and delivered by a midwife. The burial of my grandmother took place that same day. The funeral service was held in the house with burial at Wedges Prairie Cemetery near Ladoga, Wisconsin.

So here I was born to a German family, whose parents both immigrated from the Pommern area and Mecklenberg Province of Germany, located near the Baltic Sea. They all came at different times by way of Ellis Island, New York. My Grandfather August Lange worked for the New York Railroad, until he was able to save enough money so that he and my grandmother and uncle could move to a farm near the village of Waupun, Wisconsin.

The size of the original farm was about 160 acres. By the time I arrived, it had grown to over 300 acres due to the purchase of adjoining land, and some existing land a quarter of a mile along Wisconsin highway 26. The farm had a lot of potential. Crops were harvested and provided some of the income from sales of hay, grain, corn, hemp and buckwheat. Later, during World War II, major canning companies leased some of the land on shares to grow peas and sweet corn for the government. Additional amounts of grain and corn were used to feed the livestock. These sales along with milk from the dairy stock provided our income. The amount of money received depended on the open market. One had to consider the cost of fuel to run the tractors and other farm vehicles including the maintenance of all the other equipment.

The farm had various types of animals and poultry and a large herd of cattle that was made up of both mature and young stock. The poultry consisted of chickens, geese and ducks. The numbers varied. Then there were horses, which resembled the Schleswig Heavy Draft type, as well as, Quarter horses. We had one other horse that was considered a racer, named Lady Grey. I knew nothing about her until my older sister Doris told me some years later. Other than racing at the local fair, I had no knowledge that she competed in any races of notoriety. I do know that I never saw any trophies or ribbons for any of her efforts.

There were sheep with a number of new lambs born every year. Once a year the wool had to be sheared and it was baled for sale. I do know that shearing was not an easy task, but had to be done as it was part of the farm income.

So you now have a feeling of the environment I was born into. Little did I know the fun that was waiting for me, when I became old enough to enjoy the world around me.

WHEN IT ALL STARTED

To start my journey, I lived in the house with my mother, father, brother, two sisters and my paternal grandfather, August Lange. Money was scarce because times were very tough economically. Even though money was in limited supply, we had plenty of food. There was meat of all kinds including fish that we caught at the local lakes. Our large garden supplied various vegetables and fruits.

Sometimes my parents would take several dozen of eggs to the local grocer and trade them for items such as sugar, coffee and other supplies my mother needed for canning. She would can vegetables, fruit, pickles and jam made from berries or purchased peaches and cherries. The canned goods were used during the winter season. Other items such as beer and soda had to be purchased with cash. Speaking of beer, my father decided to save money by making his own. I understand that the smell almost drove everyone out of the house. This is a story for another time.

I started in the first grade at five years of age because there was no kindergarten. My school mates were all from neighboring farms. It was a one room schoolhouse and housed 28 students in the eight grades. There were three of us, two boys and one girl in the first grade.

Today with all the specialized teachers, I wonder how one teacher could possess the knowledge to prepare the students to meet the county board proficiency examinations. Somehow, we managed to learn what was necessary to graduate.

As I progressed through the grade levels, I enjoyed mathematics the most. As for the remaining subjects geography, current events, reading and maybe history I did not do badly. Spelling and grammar were a challenge.

During my early school days the county nurse came to visit and check each student's health condition. My routine eye exam revealed that I needed to have my eyes tested. A note for my parents was sent home with me. I don't know what it said, but my father did not take this very well. I am sure it was the cost for the examination and the purchase of glasses that he was not happy about. After some discussions between my parents and older sister, I was taken to have my eyes examined. Amazing how different the world looks, when you have proper vision. I always thought that everything at a distance was naturally blurry.

Willow Creek Grade School
Caption: Mrs. L. Fenelon standing in back by the glass case
Allan and Catherine in front of Mrs. Fenelon
Carolyn in seat two second row from right

One week after the glasses were issued I had the misfortune of breaking the left lens while playing on the school swing. I was lucky I didn't get glass in my eye. Breaking the glasses was not something my father wanted to hear. I offered, as my defense, that the chain from the swing snapped back and caught the lens. I still received a stern lecture and a reddened behind for the mishap. Needless to say, I can't remember a time since that mishap, that I have ever broken another pair of glasses. I am not sure whether it was the lecture or the reddened behind that instilled the life-long consciousness of protecting my glasses. Even during the time I spent in the military, my glasses remained in tact.

School presented many hours of enjoyment and challenges. One of the favorite times was recess. We had any number of games we played, but the boys favored "cowboys and Indians". One day the older boys decided I was an Indian cattle rustler, and I was judged guilty and sentenced to be hung by my neck until dead. Fashioning a hanging rope from a clothesline they put the loop around my neck. They threw the one end over the limb of a tree and began to pull me off the ground. If it wasn't for my sister Phyllis, I would not be writing this book. She saw what was happening and ran to my defense, jerked the rope from the boy's hands, and landed a few solid punches, while releasing the rope and I began breathing again. Thanks to her for prolonging my life.

SOMEONE WAS WATCHING OUT FOR ME

My sister Phyllis and I walked along a major highway to school. It was a route that ran north and south from the Illinois to the Michigan state lines. It was a highway that was traveled by many tourists. During the summer season, there was a substantial increase in traffic not only of cars and trucks, but also farm machinery.

The cars and trucks sped along at a fairly high rate of speed. One day at the age of six I was walking home from school with some of my class mates, I started across the highway toward our driveway. I glanced to the south, I didn't see any approaching vehicles. I looked north and spotted a car at some distance away. Checking once more to the south I began to cross the highway. When I got almost to the other side of the road, I was struck with a glancing blow that sent me into the bushes about fifteen feet away. Dazed and confused a man lifted me up and asked if I was hurt. I don't remember what I said and he asked again. About the same time, I heard my sister Phyllis yelling for him to put me down. He just held me and repeated the question "are you hurt?"

Then, he asked my sister where we lived, and she led him to the house while still carrying me. My mother was at the doorway and asked him what had happened. After a short conversation, she went to the phone and called the doctor. We lived about five miles from the town of Waupun and it took about twenty minutes before Dr. Swartz arrived. He checked me over and found a number of scratches, but considered me to be completely in tact with no broken bones. To this day I don't remember being hit by the car.

However, before the doctor arrived the neighbors began to call to find out what happened. Someone had listened in on my mother's call. This was a 14-party line system. When a call was made everyone knew who made the call. It sure seemed like folks were just waiting for those calls, so they could listen into the conversation.

About six weeks after the mishap, the man returned to see how I was doing. At the same time, he had a lengthy conversation with my parents.

He also asked me how I was feeling, and seemed very happy everything was going fine. He then left.

A few days later, my parents told me that the man left a sum of money for them to buy me a present. They asked me if I would like a bike or something else. I selected the something else option. I wanted a pony. About two weeks later my father took me to buy a pony. I was overjoyed.

Several months later the man came to visit us again. I thanked him and showed him the pony, "Silver". Following that visit, we never saw him again.

After the school day, it was time to do chores. I was given the task of feeding and watering the young stock, as well as the bull. A problem existed when I gave the bull a bucket of water, he insisted on pushing back and dumping it all over me. I truly hated that move. Irritated, I told my brother Jerry, and he told me to take my baseball bat and whack him between the ears as hard as I could the next time it happened. I took his advice, and did whack that bull as hard as possible.

Well, the bull sure hated me after that, and let me know it each time I came near his pen. I told my mother I was afraid of going near the bull's pen and I didn't want to water him anymore. She asked me why, and I told her what Jerry had suggested I do to solve my problem. She had a discussion with him and the task of feeding and watering the bull was eliminated from my chores.

One day an incident happened with that bull. My father always led him to the barnyard for exercise using a device that clamped to the ring in the nose of the bull. The bull decided to lunge for my father and tore the ring from his nose and knocked my father to the ground. My brother Jerry seeing what happened decided he would get the bull's attention. He climbed to the top of the barnyard fence and holding his coat over his head like the cape of Batman let out a loud roar. The bull heard this, looked around, and headed for my brother and the fence. I never saw my brother move so fast, when he leaped from the fence and ran into the barn. My father managed to crawl to another door and got inside the barn. That same day that bull was loaded into a truck and taken to the stockyard.

The purchase of my pony "Silver" instilled in me a great sense of pride. I was the envy of my classmates. One day I rode "Silver" to school. I tied her with a grazing rope so she could eat grass or lie under the shade tree, while I was in class. My classmates kept monitoring her instead of paying attention to the teacher's instructions. The teacher was not pleased about having a pony at school. She complained to my father and he told me not to take "Silver" to school again. Even as my dad told me he had a smirk on his face.

I really liked weekends. I would saddle "Silver" and ride through the fields of the farm. Sometimes I rode to a knoll and pretended it was a bluff overlooking the imaginary cattle below. Often, we would stay there for about an hour. I would just sit in the saddle with my leg over the saddle horn while "Silver" fed on the grass. It was a very peaceful time. I felt really proud because it was my horse and imaginary cattle. I tried to imagine the scene that I saw in a western book with this action. I can't say how many hours this scene would be repeated, but it sure felt good.

Allan and "Silver"

At twilight my folks milked the cows. Doris would be busy doing the house work and Phyllis helped in the barn with chores.

Grandfather would sit on the front porch and just take in the fresh air and listen to the night sounds. His eyesight was poor and he didn't venture outside without assistance. I would saddle up "Silver" and ride along the creek behind the barn and listen to the running water and other night sounds. We stopped often, while "Silver" ate the fresh grass. After about an hour, we turned around and went back to the barn to call it a night. During the summer, most evenings were spent this way.

My brother and his wife Iris lived on the farm across the highway from our farm.

One day I hitched "Silver" to my wagon and drove over to their place to take my niece Carolyn, three years younger, for a ride back to our farm. She climbed on the wagon and we drove over to my place.

After about two hours, I again hitched "Silver" to the wagon to take her home. We headed down the driveway toward the highway, we were having fun and laughing. When we reached the highway a large truck saw us and blew his air horn. The blast spooked "Silver". She whirled and took off as fast as she could run. We swung around the garage and headed straight for the open barn door. Just before we got there the wagon wheels hit something and my niece and I went tumbling out.

"Silver" ran into the barn to her stall with the bouncing empty wagon. Carolyn and I were shaking. I was so mad at "Silver" I ran into her stall and bit her ear. She glanced at me, turned her head back and went on eating some of the leftover grain, so much for my discipline tactics.

WINTER ACTIVITIES

During the winter months the farmer not only had the usual care of animals, but additionally had to keep bedding fresh, as the animals were housed inside. In summer, the cows were brought in for milking and then returned to pasture. The cleanup in the barn at that time was minimal and no bedding straw was necessary.

After the live stock had been attended to, there were machinery repair projects, each piece of equipment was investigated thoroughly and documented for their needed repairs. I, of course, went to school during this time and missed all the repair activity. I didn't like to miss what was being done, because it really fascinated me to observe how "things" came apart and then put back in operation.

My mother had often told the family members not to buy me toys, because I would only take them apart. What a reputation I achieved. The clocks had to be placed out of my reach because none were safe. If I got my hands on a clock, I would dismantle it, but never was able to reassemble it.

I was not able to ride "Silver" very often in winter because there was too much snow or ice covered with snow. I didn't want her to fall and hurt both of us. So after school, I would go home and do my required chores. By the time the evening meal was over it would be dark. All the lights were furnished by kerosene lanterns or lamps. My grandfather did not trust electricity. Since he was the owner, my father had to respect grandfather's wishes. My father tried to reason with him but there was only one answer, "no".

Sometimes at night in total darkness, I would go outside and lie on my back in the snow and peer into the heavens, and look at the thousands of stars. I wondered how they stayed up there. Were they held there with some special glue? Sunday school taught me about God in the heavens. The Sunday school teachers said God put them there. They didn't mention that he used any special glue. So that still did not answer the question as to how they were held in place. When I asked the question of my family, I was told, "the stars were there because they are, go and find something else to look at". It was a few years later that while in the seventh grade I received enough information from studying physical science that the question was answered.

Allan by the creek behind the barn in the dead of winter

Sledding and skating were activities I really enjoyed in the winter. Several of us kids would take our sleds to a nearby hill, climb to the top and cruise down while either sitting or on our stomachs. We would spend considerable time doing this with the challenge being to see who would travel the greatest distance. Whoever won would remain the champion until they were beaten on the next outing.

Skating was more of a difficult activity. We would have to locate a low place in a field, where the water from the Fall rain would have frozen. We would then clear away the snow from an area large enough on which to skate. Sometimes the creek behind the barn would freeze so we could skate back and forth for a distance of about a half mile. Although it was not very wide it still gave us hours of enjoyment.

The skates were not the shoe type you see today. These were fashioned after the roller skates of the time. A blade was set up in a way that it would hook to the back of your shoe heel. In the front a couple of clamps were hooked to the shoe sole and the clamps tightened with a key. Needless to say, that unless everything was clamped just right, it loosened and you would end up on your stomach. If you were moving fast enough you could get leveled with a "pretty good hurt".

After a couple of hours skating, we would be hungry and as always, Mother had fresh baked bread with butter and hot chocolate ready upon our arrival at the house. The kitchen had an aroma which was just out of this world. It was always warm from the large wood and coal burning stove that heated the kitchen and dining room.

A large pot belly stove located in the living room heated it, two bedrooms and the parlor. The house did not have a furnace.

The bathroom was an outhouse which in winter got pretty cold. Time was not wasted when you went there.

When it was time to go upstairs to the bedroom we would really rush. The upstairs was not heated. On severely cold evenings the stairway door was opened to let the warm air rise. It did provide a small amount of warmth. The beds always had plenty of covers. During the day, my mother would put heavy irons in the oven to warm. In the evening she would wrap them in towels and put them at the foot of the bed. This would help provide warmth, but sometime during the night they would cool, and if you touched them with your foot you did get quite a shock.

The barn and other farm buildings housing livestock and poultry were kept at a reasonable temperature by the animal body heat.

On Saturday evening my folks would often play cards with the close neighbors. They would exchange visits and my sister Phyllis and I would go along. Not my cup of tea, as they say. Their daughter and my sister were closer in age, so I was left out of their games. I would listen to the radio in one of the other rooms and fall asleep.

REN MILLER

Ren Miller was a quiet mild-mannered man. You never knew he was present. He owned the local tavern, garage, and feed and seed store, which also had a grist mill attached to the building. His building was located at the intersection of highways 26 and 103, (now TC) in Ladoga, Wisconsin. The store and tavern were located about 2 miles from our farm. On the northeast corner my folk's niece Violet and her husband, Melvin Wilkerson, owned the grocery store. There was a grange hall about a city block from the tavern and feed store. These were the only buildings at the intersection.

Periodically during the month, the local farmers would meet at the tavern to talk shop so to speak. The discussions centered on the crop rotations and what seed they needed to purchase from Ren. Since he owned the community thrashing machine, a tentative schedule would be diagramed with each farmers name and the number of days he might need the equipment. Basically, the schedule didn't change except when a rain caused a day's cancellation of one farmer's harvest. The schedule was fairly easy to set up. Based on when each farmer planted his grain, and the days required for germination, a time could be established and Ren could bring the thrashing equipment.

Often on Saturday night my dad, brother and I would head for Ladoga or "Dog Town" as it was called, to converse and drink beer, or soda in my case. Usually I was the only kid there, so it was rather boring. We would stay for about two hours and then take the five minute trip home.

When my mother and sisters would go along with us they would spend the time visiting with Violet, who lived across the road. Violet and Melvin lived in an apartment upstairs above their grocery store. I don't believe my mother ever went into Ren's Tavern, because she didn't like the condition of the place. If there would have been a health inspection, Ren would have been closed for an eternity. My father would go there to make payments on whatever business transactions he had made during the month. If one was looking for local color, that would be the place to visit. During the winter, the tavern still had its customers. The farmers would bring grain or corn to the grist mill to be ground up and bagged as feed for the livestock. Ren had a good business year around.

The Ladoga Grange Hall was an old church moved from a location across from the Wedges Prairie Cemetery, which was located about three miles west of Ladoga. The hall was a place that held a number of community activities. On Sunday after church, my folks would drive home and have lunch and in the afternoon we would drive to Ladoga for "the big Bingo Game". My mother loved to play bingo. She and my dad would go to the game, and my sisters and I would stay home, older sister Doris would be in charge. She was the one who spent a lot of time with me. When my folks were busy with the farm work, I would spend time by myself or with her. Phyllis was busy with her playmates and I was in the way, as younger brothers often are. So Doris had to keep me out of trouble, which I was famous for getting into. There wasn't much I wouldn't do which sometimes caused me harm. Today, I still have a number of scars to prove it caused by barbed wire, pitchforks, climbing trees, and playing with jackknives.

SUMMER TIME AND THE LIVING WASN'T EASY

As winter faded to spring and the weather warmed the earth, the Wisconsin farmer began to organize the tasks for the summer months ahead.

During the fall months of October and part of November the individual farmer had plowed as much of the land as the weather allowed. Much depended on the rainfall and whether there was an early frost. The plowing was done during this time to give him a head start on the spring crop planting.

The first crops to be planted were the different grains such as oats, wheat, rye and barley. Following the grain was the corn planting. Most of this work was finished in mid-June. From mid-June thru mid-July the hay fields were cut and gathered into the barn for feeding the live stock in winter.

Prior to the invention of the hay baler equipment, the hay was cut using a mower system. This system had a seven foot arm which housed an oscillating blade. To cut the hay it was lowered, and as the mower was pulled by horses or tractor through the field, it would cut a swath of grass that would be left to dry for a couple of days. Then the six foot plus swaths would be raked into a roll ready for loading onto a wagon.

Once the hay was rolled into long rows, a team of horses were hitched to a wagon with the loader equipment, which straddled the row and the loader would sweep the hay onto the wagon. Either my father or brother would be on the wagon and directed the hay for a uniform load. My sister Phyllis or I would drive the horses. When the wagon was full, the loader would be unhooked and the loaded wagon would be taken to the barn.

At the barn, a system of ropes and pulleys with a large fork would be lowered to the load of hay. The fork would be set into the hay and with me leading a horse hooked to the rope of the pulley system, the fork filled with hay would be pulled up the side of the barn and once it reached the track that traversed through the center of the barn, it would be pulled inside. When the fork of hay reached the right location my brother, Jerry, would yell "pull". My father would pull the fork catch rope and the hay would fall into the barn. This process was repeated until the wagon was empty. Then it was back to the field for another load. When the fields were finished the barn was full.

Mid-July represented a start of the cash crop harvest. This was the crop of peas planted on the land leased by the major canning company, and they would be busy performing about the same processes as used for hay harvest. The work was done by their employees and it was finished by the time the farmers were ready to harvest grain.

The grain was cut with a piece of equipment pulled by a team of horses or tractor. When the grain was cut an apron system carried the grain up through a mechanical tying system that formed it and tied the bundles. Once the cutting was finished the bundles would be stacked neatly into shocks. Now the grain was ready to be loaded on a wagon to be hauled to the thrashing machine.

Brother Jerry and the grain binder

Ren Miller would be contacted and he would transport his thrashing machine to the farm. The neighboring farmers would arrive with their wagons and began loading the grain bundles. They would haul the loaded wagons to the thrashing machine and fork off the bundles into the thrasher. There, grain would be separated from the straw. An elevator would take the grain and dump it into a waiting truck that would haul it to the granary. This effort was repeated for each farm in the area.

The introduction of the combine after World War II made each farmer more independent. It changed the farming community completely. The farmer became more productive, but the bonds that had developed between neighbors faded. It was the beginning of the larger farms and the small farmer was losing out. Today the agribusiness has displaced most of the small farms in the state. It is sad to see that way of life, as I knew it, become extinct.

Grandfather August, father, Edward and Allan looking over the grain shocks

Mom (Esther), Ren Miller and Dad (Edward) on thrashing machine

Front:Ted Mittelstaedt, Art Damrow and Allan
Back: George Tourtellotte at the bags, Ren Miller standing on top of the thrasher and Dad (Edward) holding his hat in the air, his customary "Hello" signal.

HARVEST LABORERS

During the harvest season there was more work than the family could handle. Often my parents would take on a "hired hand". Usually, it was someone that was known around the community. Generally, these were individuals who had been displaced because of the Depression. They traveled in and out of the state in search of work. These men were provided room and board plus a weekly salary. I, for one, enjoyed their company. They had stories to tell.

Sometimes in the evening when the work for the day was completed, they would tell me their tales of jumping the freight trains in search for the next job. At times, they would have to spend it in a hobo camp relying on other people for help. Some even traveled south to work as an animal caretaker for "Barnum and Bailey Circus". Each hired hand had his stories. True or not, I didn't care, I loved them.

December 7, 1941 changed the farm labor picture. Many of the men for hire joined or were drafted by the military and the farmers were left without labor assistance. To offset this problem, my father wrote the Draft Board and was able to get my brother deferred.

There was still a need in the area for help. Thankfully, the canning company was able to convince the government to allow them to bring workers from Mexico. Soon the families arrived, who had also experienced the trials of the Depression and were put into temporary camp areas. Somehow my father was able to persuade the canning company to convert an old vacant cheese factory into living quarters for some of these workers. The cheese factory was not far from our farm. The conversion was rather easy as only dividers had to be placed for family separation. The bathroom facilities were shared. Even though many did not speak English, it all worked out.

I remember one incident when a woman came running to our house and tried to explain a problem. Somewhere in the conversation the words son and sick were understood. My father called the family doctor, Dr. Kenneth Swartz, and he came rushing to the farm. My family and the doctor were concerned about the nature of the illness. Of course, it could be anything, and they hoped it wasn't contagious. So the doctor, my father and the woman went to the cheese factory quarters.

After the doctor examined the teenage boy, he determined it was appendicitis. The boy needed an operation. The mother was beside herself. How was she to pay for the operation? My father convinced the doctor to go ahead and he would help pay the bill.

Dad explained to the leader of the workers, what had to be done, and that they needed to load the boy into the doctor's car and take him to the hospital. The leader and the boy went with the doctor in his car, and my dad and the boy's mother went in our car. Later, when the boy healed, the leader and the boy's family came to our house to thank my father. Eventually the bill was shared by my father, the canning factory and the doctor.

At the end of the harvest season, and as the workers were about to go back to Mexico, the boy's mother visited my parents. Not much was said except for "gracias", which was repeated many times with handshakes all around. Then the woman presented my mother with a quilt she had made from scraps of cloth, she had collected. A gesture of considerable appreciation for all that my folks had done for her family.

Also during the war, when I was about nine, the government brought German prisoners to America to provide the labor to help with the harvest. Around fifteen prisoners worked on our farm. The major canning company used them to help harvest the peas, sweet corn and lima beans. The company asked the farmers to provide the noon meal which everyone did gladly.

Many of the German speaking farmers in the area refused the prisoners, because they were afraid that they would be accused of being unpatriotic. However, my folks agreed to the prisoner help and also spoke their language. During conversations they learned a great deal about Germany and the prisoners' feelings. Some paid attention to me because I reminded them of their family back home.

There was never any problem with the prisoners. Many of the German prisoners were very young. Like most Americans, they just wanted peace, and to get on with their lives.

The meals cooked by my mother and other farmers wives were really enjoyed, as it reminded them of food they ate at home. Sometimes some prisoners would breakdown and cry. That left a lasting impression on me. War sure takes its toll.

At the end of each day the prisoners would be taken back to the local camp located near the state prison in Waupun. There they spent the evening in tents, and were brought back under guard the next day. My folks often remarked how well mannered they were.

THE WAR YEARS

As the war years progressed, a new crop, hemp, was introduced to the farmers by the government. The fibers were to be used for the production of rope for the war effort. To assist the farmers, a government representative was sent to instruct the farmers on the planting and harvesting of the crop. I was told that I should never take any of the plant in my mouth, as it would make me crazy. I always made sure to keep my mouth tightly closed when near the plants. It was mystifying to me, and only years later did I find out it has another name, "marijuana".

Once the plants were fully grown they were harvested much like the grain. Six foot swaths were cut and left to dry for about two weeks or until the stalks had turned completely black. The stalks were picked up by a piece of equipment similar to a grain binder and tied in bundles. The bundles were placed onto a truck and hauled about five miles to the hemp factory. Here it was mashed to remove the pulp and the fibers were wound onto a mandrel to be shipped to another factory. The second factory would treat the fibers and twist them into a rope. The pulp could be used for livestock bedding material much like straw was used.

At the end of the war, the factory was closed and hemp was never raised legally in the area again.

As World War II raged on, the farming community was kept busy raising the food and supportive crops for the country and the military.

Rationing was placed on gasoline and all food stuffs. When people could not meet their required needs, because they did not have enough rationing stamps allotted, other neighbors would help out. Often people would access the telephone party line system to contact those willing to barter with their stamps. It all worked reasonably well.

For a sort of get away from it all, once a month in the summer on Saturday evening there would be a movie shown. A big white barn in the area served as the screen. The movies were rented from the county office. All the neighbors would gather at the farm and bring their own snacks and drinks. At about 9pm or when it was very dark, the movie would start. They were old movies and there was no sound system. Most of them I remember were westerns. Everyone watched and ate the goodies with a sense of relaxation and enjoyed the break in the routine. A lot of the older folks just spent the time off to the side in friendly conversation. I think the movies were for the children and kept them occupied to give the parents some free time.

THE HEMP FACTORY 1940's
Taken from the Waupun Leader News October 27, 1976

As the months passed slowly by, my sister Doris, received only a few letters from her boy friend, Harvey. These letters were made of very thin paper known as V-mail. All letters were censored which often cut words or sentences. She never knew where he was located and that kept her worried. It wasn't until he was discharged that the locations were ever revealed.

In February 1944, farming changed for my parents. My grandfather, August Lange Sr., passed away at the family farm. It was a sad time. He was confined to his bed for the last 2 years of his life. He could not walk, and his vision was blurred. His life was confined to one room with my parents and two sisters caring for him. In fact, it basically confined the family to the farm, as we couldn't go anyplace as a family. It really required two people to stay at home at all times. So our visits with the other relatives were limited to namely them coming to see us.

The funeral was conducted from our home with the eulogy given at the house, and then the burial at the nearby Wedges Prairie Cemetery near Ladoga, Wisconsin. During the eulogy, I somehow became the center of attention, when after a long service that seemed to take forever.

I said "isn't he done yet" to my sister Phyllis. This got me a rather lengthy lecture from both my parents. However, it did bring a snicker from the attendees.

The death of my grandfather gave my parents concern because the farm belonged to my grandfather and would probably go to the eldest son William. What would my parents do? They would probably have to move to another farm somewhere. Not an easy thing to do during war time. So they would have to wait for the will to go to probate. It wasn't a long wait.

About a week after grandfather's death, the lawyer summoned my parents and my two uncles and their wives to his office. It was announced that my father, Edward, would inherit the farm. This brought about a flurry of activity on the part of my uncles, as they wanted to contest the will. They contacted lawyers and started to argue that my parents corrupted my grandfather into giving the farm to my father, even though they each had their own farm.

In the final hearings some weeks later, the uncles lost and my father won. My parents were happy but sorry that the whole process caused such bitterness. The uncles were to each receive a sum of money from my father.

The value of the farm was determined by a county appraiser for tax purposes, and the amount due each uncle was determined by the appraised amount.

They still were not happy and very angered at the outcome. As a result, my father had to auction everything but a few head of livestock and some equipment to make the payments. After the dust settled, my uncles did not speak to my father for years.

After about 20 plus years my dad's oldest brother, William suffered a tragic accident in his family. A granddaughter suffered severe burns from pulling a pot of scalding water over her and after about a week she passed away. My father and mother went to the funeral and my uncle finally shook hands with my father and said he was sorry for his actions. The other uncle, August, never did speak to my father for the rest of his life.

Now it was time for my parents to start over.

Caption: *Left to right: Edward, August Jr., William Lange*
Seated: August Lange Sr. 1940's

A NEW BEGINNING

Confused and hurt by the events of Grandfather Lange's passing, my parents gathered their thoughts and started reconstructing their life. As a result it brought about a new beginning for my sisters and me.

Armed with the ownership of the farm, an assortment of equipment, livestock, and money left over from the auction, my folks began planning the road to recovery.

On a handshake, my father borrowed a minimum amount of money from the local bank to buy livestock and farm machinery. The earlier sale of the livestock meant there was extra land available to rent to the local canning company. My father entered into a rental contract with the company for two years. He figured it would take him that long to rebuild the herd of livestock to the original numbers.

The rental money provided additional income that was used to install electricity. A cow milking system was also installed, which would reduce the milking time by 80 percent. In addition, the need to clean and trim the wicks on the kerosene lamps was eliminated.

Until my mother had her washing machine converted to an electric motor, it had a gasoline engine. One always knew when she was washing by the familiar (and loud) "putt-putt" of the gasoline engine's exhaust coming from the pipe that was placed out of the basement window. With the electric motor no sound or fumes filled the basement, which was a big improvement.

My father traveled to every auction within a one hundred mile radius to obtain equipment and livestock. I remember the purchase he made of a cultivator that was like new. He bragged to my mother that he had really got a good deal for the price. When he had it delivered it was placed next to the storage shed. I saw a beautiful piece of equipment and just could not resist the temptation to take it apart.

I removed a couple of nuts and bolts, and a pair of heavy springs flew in different directions. I tried and tried but just couldn't reassemble the spring system. When my father saw what I did, I received a sore behind from his straight razor strap. It took about half a day for my father and brother to reassemble the cultivator.

A couple of weeks later on a visit to my Aunt Laura and Uncle Paul's house, I mentioned it to my uncle. He suggested that I bury the razor strap. Fantastic idea! I did just that when we returned home.

Some weeks later on a return trip to their house, my father mentioned to my uncle, that he couldn't find his good razor strap. My uncle thought for a moment then burst into laughter. My father looked puzzled at my uncle and wanted to know what was so funny. My uncle told him of my conversation about the strap, and that he told me to bury the strap. After a few words, they both laughed. I never had a problem with any other disciplinary actions or a sore behind again. Life was good.

As the warmest season of the year faded into fall, and winter began to start its reign, my father decided to raise some additional money by trapping for furs. We had a number of muskrat and mink animals that lived along the creek banks. So he set his traps and made a fair sum of money with the pelts that he obtained. He would catch the prey and if they did not die during the evening he would shoot them. He then would bring them home and remove the skin, and stretch it over a piece of thin wood, then dry it in the sun and air.

Once the skin was dry he would take it to the local fur trader and obtain his money. Once he caught a skunk. The skunk won. Before my father could shoot the animal it released its spray and nailed my father. On returning home, my mother must have got a whiff and told my father to remove his clothes, bury them and wash completely a couple of times with some fairly strong soap. If you are wondering why they did not use tomato juice, well it wasn't available in sufficient quantity. The skunk pelt brought a fair price.

My parents continued to work hard at restocking the farm. During 1945 it was almost back to the original number prior to the auction. Our life, however, was about to change again.

THE END OF WORLD WAR II

The old saying of "it is always darkest before dawn" was a good description of the mood in the country. Was there ever going to be an end to the war?

For several weeks our family worried about the battles that were taking place. My sister, Doris, was worried about her boy friend, Harvey, because she had not received a letter from him for a couple of months. The weeks dragged on as the allied forces were advancing on all fronts in Europe, and General MacArthur was headed back to invade the Philippines. There was still no word from Harvey. We later learned that Harvey fought in the Pacific. He took part in battles that ousted the Japanese from Australia, and New Guinea and was part of the invasion of the Philippines. Ironically, Harvey had enlisted in the Army on April 17, 1941 during a recruitment drive in Wisconsin. After three or four months of training, he was assigned to the 32nd Tank Destroyer unit. (Their patch was a panther crushing a tank). He was on a convoy going across country to be shipped overseas to Germany, when the Japanese attacked Pearl Harbor. The convoy was ordered to turn around and proceed to the West Coast to be shipped to the Pacific war zone.

On the home front, my father kept buying livestock and farm equipment. He kept doing everything he could to keep the supply of grain, corn, buckwheat, hemp and peas flowing to the government buyers. Time dragged on. Routines were followed with a focused purpose. Then the first real good news was received, Harvey was returning to the states after a continuous thirty three months in the South Pacific corridor. However, we didn't know where he would dock. We received a telephone call in January 1945, that he had docked in San Francisco. A week later another call from him said that he had chicken pox and would be quarantined for 2 weeks.

Harvey finally came home February 9th and the wedding that had been tentatively planned between the 9th and the 17th.

A flurry of activity ensued. Doris had to buy her wedding dress. Due to the war effort, there was a problem with getting one. A call was made to Edith's Shop in Fond du Lac, Wisconsin and luckily a shipment of wedding dresses had just come in, Doris was able to buy a dress. Everyone was happy.

My father had to go to the cold storage locker and collect enough beef and pork roasts in order to supply the meat for the wedding reception dinner. That about took care of the meat supply the folks had reserved for the remaining winter months. We would just have to eat more chicken. Anyway, the meal and the dance afterwards went very well.

The wedding day was February 17th, 1945 and the temperature was 20 degrees below zero. They were married at the Immanuel Lutheran Church in Waupun, Wisconsin, followed by the dinner. After the dinner everyone drove back to our farm for dancing and drinks.

Doris (Lange) and Harvey Rahn
and niece Carolyn Lange
February 17, 1945

For me it was the gaining of a brother-in-law who would turn out to be a life long buddy. We just seemed to click. I could really talk to him. Sometimes I would ask him about the war, but he just told me he really didn't want to talk about it. Although he did tell me that while his outfit was in New Guinea a group of his buddies thought it would be nice for the guys to have some fresh meat. So they shot a water buffalo. Unfortunately, they had such a hard time trying to skin it that they decided to shoot a younger one. This provided the fresh meat. The natives were not happy, but finally let it pass.

In the meantime, my parents decided to convert our large house into two apartments. My parents and I would live in the upstairs apartment and Doris and Harvey would live down stairs.

My father then decided to purchase the neighboring farm. This would allow my brother to have a farm of his own someday, and Doris and Harvey would share the homestead with my folks. Jerry and Harvey were to work together and my father would help both of them. Again, life was really good.

The Japanese War was officially over when the surrender was signed on September 2, 1945.

When I entered school in the fall of 1945, I had a new teacher. Her name was Mrs. Loretta Fenelon. I liked her from the start. Why, I really can't tell you, but my instincts were right. With her help, I was able to master some advanced mathematics that really helped me on the final exams to graduate the seventh and eight grades. Either my previous teachers only taught the basics or they didn't have the knowledge to provide the principles for the more advanced material. In the long run, it influenced and encouraged me to make mathematics a part of my career.

A TIME TO LET GO

Sometime when I was between the ages of 10 and 11, my father rescued a couple of small piglets from two litters. These small runts would have not lived because they were being aced out of the feeding process. My father gathered them up and handed them to me. He said that I had the responsibility of feeding and caring for them. So that is what I did.

These small creatures had to be fed several times a day from a bottle with a nipple and warmed cow's milk. This continued for several weeks until they were old enough to wean off the milk and given solid food. To train them, I had to mix some ground grain in a bowl of warm milk. I had to dip their nose in the bowl and try to at least get them to open their mouth, and hopefully take in some of the mixture. After several days it started to work and they began to eat.

I spent so much time with them that when they were let out of their pen they would follow me and make all kind of squeals. They would follow me everywhere.

I remember once I took the piglets into the house. Was that the wrong thing to do. It is the first time I had ever heard my mother curse. She yelled, "Get those damn pigs out of the house". The piglets beat me to the door and tumbled down the steps. I will say, I never did that again.

As they ate everything in sight including fruits and vegetables, as well as the grain, they grew. Boy, did they grow. About a year and a half later they topped 300 pounds. Unfortunately, it was time to send them to market. A very sad day for me, it was like losing two old buddies.

When you grow up on a farm there is one thing you learn young, you can have farm animals, but don't get attached to them, because as time goes by, you know what the results are going to be. To make a living in farming, you must learn that you can enjoy certain things, and then you must let go.

In the summer of 1945, I was eleven years old. It was a time when my constant companion "Silver", was too small for me to ride. My feet would almost touch the ground when I took her for an outing. So the frequency of our expeditions decreased. Because of the inactivity, she began to gain weight. My father mentioned that, maybe, I should sell her to some family with children, who would enjoy having her to ride. I would not hear of it.

One Sunday I had her tethered in a grassy area close to the main highway. A family happened to drive by and saw her. They stopped by the house and inquired of my father if she was for sale. Father told the man that he would have to ask me. I said "no", but I thought about it all the next week. He had two smaller children, a boy and a girl, that were about the age that I was when I purchased "Silver".

The following Sunday the family returned, and asked me if I would change my mind and sell the pony. Again I said "no". It would be extremely difficult for me to part with her. The man left his phone number and told me to call if I changed my mind. They asked if they could see her once more and if his children could pet her. I agreed. Those kids really liked "Silver" and she liked them. She enjoyed all the attention. It was something I hadn't been doing much of lately. They left and I thought about it again.

About the middle of the following week I called and told the man that I would sell her and named the price. He agreed and said that in two weeks they would come by and pick her up. I had never experienced any feeling like that before. I think I cried on and off for about a week. I was lonesome to the core of my being.

I purchased a bicycle about two months after I sold her. The bike became a mechanical "Silver" for me. I never forgot that pony and the pleasures we shared. I never heard another word about her again.

It was a time to let go.

THE FALL HARVEST

The farmers in Wisconsin grew two distinct types of corn. There is one type called "field" corn that was used for livestock feed. The second type was the "sweet" corn for the canning companies. The ears of the "sweet" corn were picked from the stalk by hand and loaded on a truck that took them to the canning factory. The kernels were stripped from the corn cob, cooked and canned.

The remaining stalks from the sweet corn, my father cut and tied in a bundle with the equipment fashioned like that used to harvest the grain. It was called a corn binder. The bundles were then cut up by a piece of equipment called a silo filler. The chopped stalks were often combined with a crop called sorghum. The combination is very rich and the cattle loved it. One problem, if they ate too much, bloating could occur and this could take the life of a cow if severe. So it was monitored with close measured feeding. The food does influence the amount of milk that a cow produces.

The "field corn" had to be processed differently. The stalks were cut and tied into a bundle with the corn binder. The bundles were then stacked in shocks that resembled wigwams.

The corn stalks were processed through the corn shredder. Ren Miller owned the corn shredder and at a local meeting in Ladoga, the schedule dates for each farmer was decided.

Once the corn was shredded the ears were ready for the corn cribs. The stored ear corn would be used for feed for the livestock. The shredded stalks would be used for bedding for the livestock. When processed through the shredder the corn stalks would be pulverized enough for good bedding.

A certain amount of the "field" corn would also be processed through the silo filler and mixed with the "sweet" corn stalks and sorghum that provided some base to tone down this rich mixture, which was fed to the cows.

To pick the "sweet" corn ears the canning company hired migrant workers from Jamaica. I remember one year that my father had several fields of "sweet" corn that needed picking. It was a wet and dreary day. The Jamaicans did not want to work, because it was so wet. My father was beside himself, as he needed the income from the canning company to meet the bills. If the corn was not picked, it would rot and the schedule for picking the neighboring fields would not allow for a delay. He talked to the foreman, and asked "if I furnish your men with some beer and a bottle of rum, will they pick the corn"? As they picked the corn, the beautiful songs rang out. After a while I joined in the choruses. The day flew by and the corn was picked.

Allan, Mom (Esther) Dad (Edward) with a Silo filler and partial load of corn

Mom, (Esther), Dad (Edward), Allan, Phyllis and Jerry pulling Allan's Hair

All the work surrounding the harvest of the corn has now changed considerably. The "sweet" corn ears are picked by equipment. The sounds of the Jamaican songs are gone. The "field" corn is now processed by corn choppers with the fodder blown into a screened wagon or truck and hauled to the barn where a large blower carries the processed corn into the silo.

The advanced equipment used for harvesting the crops raised by the farms today has in many ways taken some of the spirit away, that I remember, and the real meaning of neighbors working together, no matter the challenge.

MY NEW CHALLENGE

September rolled around and I was faced with a new challenge. I was going into the seventh grade in public school and my folks enrolled me in the Saturday church doctrine or Catechism class at the Immanuel Lutheran Church of Waupun, Wisconsin. The church was the one that my grandparents, parents and other relatives were members. In fact, my grandfather had a helping hand in the construction effort of the church. The church has been designated as a state historical site because of the beautiful stained glass windows that were imported from Germany.

When I started the church instruction I ran into some problems with understanding some of the concepts of just accepting what we were taught. Some of it just didn't "click upstairs" with me. I had developed in my own mind the concept of God. He was a friend that I could talk to at anytime day or night. Now suddenly, I had to perform some type of worship that needed to have certain criteria met just to converse in the form of "prayer or prayers". Gee, I thought you could just carry on a conversation without a lot of formality. What a change. He suddenly became this "King" in the sky we all had to bow to. This sure puzzled me.

In school we studied a number of subjects and somehow I could not connect the relationship between the subjects, and that of the church doctrine classes. One day I happened to mention this connection problem to Mrs. Fenelon. She pointed out that in order to understand God, we needed to study the laws of the land and how these laws relate to God's order of things. She also pointed out that the social studies area was associated with living with others on earth. Mathematics provided the insight of how the universe functioned. Mathematics also provided the language that allows us all to communicate with one language. Well, this was pretty heavy stuff.

The battle within me continued and I tried to put it out of my mind, and just believe in having my usual conversations with God. In the doctrine classes, I just recited what I had to. In the regular school, I studied and did the best I could. Soon Mrs. Fenelon saw that I was pretty good at mathematics. She added extra work after school and instruction into more advanced material. I loved it and soon forgot the other problem with church and school.

THE IMMANUEL LUTHERAN CHURCH OF WAUPUN, WISCONSIN

(A COPY OF A METAL PLATE THAT HUNG IN GRANDMOTHER'S KITCHEN)

Somewhere in the middle of all this study, my father talked to me about becoming a minister. He added this zinger from left field. I never gave it any consideration until he said one day "son, you must become something other than a farmer, as it is a life fast fading as we know it". "You should become a minister". I hadn't thought I would ever be anything other than a farmer. Although I didn't much like the farm work, I just thought that was it. Suddenly there was a new idea to dwell upon. What in heck did a minister do?

So I once again approached Mrs. Fenelon with my question of "what does a minister do"? She explained very completely that I would have to go to college and find out the major duties of a minister. What was college? The idea of another school really intrigued me, but I wasn't sure about the minister idea. But she explained I had to go to high school first, so I had to study hard and get good marks on the county board exams. She now spent a considerable amount of time with me and my studies. Sometimes she would come to our house and tutor me. I found out only two of us students even thought of college and the other classmate was Catherine Nietman, an 8th grader.

Catherine and I were close friends and spent a considerable amount of time together during the year. She was very interesting to talk to and we often spent time discussing our future. She wanted to be a school teacher, which she later became. I still wasn't sure that I would like being a minister. She said I should try it, and maybe I could change when I found something I liked. Now I tried to focus on the challenge of a career as a minister, when I grew up.

Certainly with the help of Mrs. Fenelon I did well on the county exams and moved on into the 8th grade. I finished the first year of church school and it was not hard to just recite what I had to, in order to move to the next level.

THE FOUR-H CLUB

During the summer of 1946, at the age of 12, my folks thought that it would be nice for me to become a member of a club called 4-H or Four-H. The club meetings were held every Sunday evening in the Grange Hall at Ladoga, Wisconsin. They would drive me to the meeting and listen in on the proceedings. The truth be known, it wasn't exactly what I wanted to do, but when they wanted me to do something, I did it, but not without a bit of resistance.

The 4-H's stood for head, heart, hands and health. A government grant started the clubs in the farming communities across the country. The grant was originally provided by the Smith-Lever Act of 1914. Private support stepped in about 1921. The idea was to encourage rural students to incorporate farm experiment studies along with their other studies. It was a good idea and a large number of young people were involved with the activities. Once I started getting involved I found it to be kind of enjoyable.

My experiment was to take a young calf about five months old and feed the animal a mixture of grains and clover to see how it would develop along with the others that were given their normal mixtures. It sounded good, but where was I going to get a mixture that would be totally different.

Dad must have had that figured out before the meeting and he thought it was a good idea. So when we left the meeting I asked him, "where in the world do I get something different to feed the calf". He said "remember how you fed the two pigs the chicken feed and how well they grew, let's try it with the calf". I guess he was right, but I thought there wasn't much difference from the ordinary stuff fed the other animals.

He told me to look at the bag of chicken feed and write down the names of the ingredients the mixture contained. Also, we will make a comparison list of what the other livestock received. I did just that and although I don't remember the differences, the 4-H leader liked the idea when I showed him my comparison list.

The summer flew by and I fed and brushed that calf everyday.

The real test came when I had to train the calf to the head halter. There was a real test of will between the calf and myself. My father helped me train the calf and after several attempts it worked. She now could be led around the farm yard and was very gentle. The training to the halter was necessary so that when I had to show her at the county fair, the judge could be assured that he could check her over completely. This required a lot of practice time and frequent stops during the walk to be examined. My mother would help out with the complete check of teeth, limbs, eyes and hooves. At first, the calf was very touchy but over time she expected the exam and all went well.

In late August the fair was held and we had to load the calf in the trailer and haul her to the fair grounds in Fond du Lac, which was 15 miles away. The trip went well and we were able to find a nice stall at the stock barn to house her for the week event. Once the calf was secured in the stall, my parents and I went out to enjoy some of the other fair festivities.

When evening arrived, I had to find a place to sleep near the calf so that I could be handy in case attention was required. Finding a place on a couple of bales of straw, I spread out my blanket and when the lights were dimmed I went to sleep. When my parents visited the next day they asked me where I had slept. I took them to the place and they were stunned. The two bales of straw were parked neatly between two young bulls. My mother became a bit upset and immediately searched for a safer place for me to sleep. I ended up a bit farther from my calf, but the straw bed was comfortable.

In the morning I got up, went to the public showers, new to me, learned the use of it and proceeded to get ready for the daily activities. It was time to feed and brush the calf and then go for breakfast. I met a lot of other boys and girls about my age. This routine went on for a week.

Each experiment was registered with the fair commission and a day for review of the project was assigned. I was scheduled to show my calf and describe my project to the judge. After a complete review of each category, prizes were given out. I received a second place award of a red ribbon and $5. I was very excited, when I met my parents and showed them the results of my efforts with the calf. They were very happy for me.

The judging completed, it was now time to load up the calf in the trailer and take it back home. There it was returned to join the other group of young stock.

Shortly after the fair, the folks asked me if I would like to try another project. "Do I have to"? I asked. They decided that I had enough of the club, so I never went back to the meetings.

THE FAMILY

The family was changing in numbers. My brother, Jerry, had married in 1937.

Iris (Thalacker) and Gerald Lange
April 23, 1937

My sister, Doris, was married in February 1945. My sister, Phyllis, married in September 1945, at the young age of 17. That left me with my parents, to receive the largest share of attention.

Jerry and his wife, Iris, had a second daughter, Betsy, in 1942. In 1944 their son Orlin was born. Doris and husband Harvey had a son, Darrell, born in 1946. This now meant that a larger group gathered at the family holiday dinners at my parent's house. It was considered too much work for my mother alone, so the others cooked a dish of food and brought it to the dinners. What a feast we had. When the meal was finished the women cleaned up the dishes and the men talked about farm work. Often disagreements came up, but they would cease when the women walked into the room. The children were left to find things to do.

My oldest niece, Carolyn, and I usually went outside to play with the animals. The younger ones stayed in the house and played with their toys.

During the summer of 1946 at the age of 12, I was recruited by my father to work with my brother Jerry at his place located just a quarter of a mile down the road from the homestead, where we lived with Doris and Harvey. My father decided he would help Harvey. As the summer progressed, I was having problems working for Jerry. He didn't think I could do anything right and let me know about it constantly. I told my father about the problem, so he decided to switch with me and he would work with Jerry, and I would work with Harvey. Harvey was a lot of fun to work with. I did hear from time to time about the problems he had working with my father, so it all seemed to work out much better with this arrangement.

When September arrived I returned to school the day after Labor Day. The day I started eighth grade, Mrs. Fenelon asked me about my summer vacation experiences, and I told her about my problem working with my brother. She told me not to concern myself about it, as she was sure it wasn't me he was mad at, it was just the frustrations about all the work that had to be done. I felt better about the situation and sure enough about a week later he treated me to a hamburger and acted as though nothing had happened. I thought Mrs. Fenelon was the wisest person in the world.

The first Saturday after Labor Day I started my second year of church doctrine. More memorizing of things not really understood but retained. I had the ability to memorize the principles. I must have gotten that ability from my mother's genes.

She often recited poems or songs that she had learned in school. An example of one writing was Edgar Allan Poe's "The Raven". She would recite it with real feeling. She liked the work of Poe so much that she decided to call me Allan. Longfellow's, "The Village Smithy", was another favorite of hers. She never missed a word or verse. I would sit in front of her and she would recite those poems or sing a song while she peeled the vegetables. I sat there in awe. So with her coaching, I could recite the doctrine phrases, when called upon to do so by the minister in class.

Over the years my folks had become good friends with the minister and his wife. During the fall, my father was elected to serve as the church council president. This turned up the heat on me to become a minister. Good grief, things weren't bad enough for me, the church council decided to send me to a Christian Leadership class over the Thanksgiving weekend. I had more memorization to do without the understanding of what it all meant.

A week after the training, I had to appear before the council and tell them about my experience. I was shaking in my shoes. Bless my mother, she helped me prepare and I guess I did well enough, as they thought I knew my stuff. I should have become an actor.

l-r: Carolyn, Esther, Edward (holding Darrell)
standing in front: Orlin and Betsy (late 1940's)

DEALING WITH THE PROBLEMS

As Christmas of 1946 approached the uneasy air of Harvey's dealings with the work on the farm and my father were causing problems. They were having numerous arguments. Doris tried to be the peace maker but it didn't work. By spring, he was looking for another farm to work on shares. I was a bit rattled by the events but kept quiet. I went to school and attended the church doctrine class on Saturdays. So my world was filled with my own problems. Dealing with questions of science and its connection with religion was no small effort.

I really enjoyed the daily routine at school. Mrs. Fenelon always had something new for us. Sometimes she would tell or read us a story. Once in a while she would have the eighth graders read a story to be selected by the reader from a list she provided. Everyone enjoyed our 8:00am start of school. The time period for the song or reading usually covered the first 15 minutes and then it was down to the daily lessons.

She usually would ask someone to select a number from one to eight, of course, representing the grades. The number taken would be the starting grade for the daily lessons. It continued in that rotation until the following day when a new number would be selected. Sometimes it could be a repeat. For some reason I always liked being first. The day just seemed to run more smoothly for me. Maybe it was because I was a morning person. I was born early in the morning and have maintained that early morning "up and at 'um" routine for 76 years. I enjoy the solitude of listening to the morning sounds or their absence, because it is so peaceful. It is the time I feel the closest to God.

Each day was started with a different subject. I guess in this way Mrs. Fenelon felt we wouldn't get bored. School meant a variety of daily activities and that was good.

The fall months allowed us to play softball. We had a good team. There were four other schools like ours located in adjoining townships. Games were scheduled where we would sometimes travel to another school in an afternoon for a very competitive contest. The travel would be provided by the volunteer parents. It was an afternoon of fun and refreshments, that were again, provided by the parents of the host school. I usually played center field and was a reasonably good hitter. I had a small frame, but could run very well and often beat out a ground ball for a base hit. Base stealing was not legal, so my skill was not challenged.

I can't say there was any one game that provided more challenge over others. The scores were close and the games were played with a lot of vocal enthusiasm. By the time the cold weather arrived, we would have played the other four schools. The spring months of April and May again provided weather for the softball games. I enjoyed the sport and the competitive spirit of the games.

School winter activities were mainly composed of craft projects that we could give our parents for Christmas. Depending on your age, the craft projects varied. I don't recall any of the things I ever created for my parents. The time spent on the project usually occupied about an hour a day for four or five weeks. Mrs. Fenelon had a large selection from which to choose. I really needed only a small amount of assistance so she helped those with problems. Outside fun usually ended up in a snowball fight between the boys and girls. The winner of the fight was never declared, but each side claimed victory.

Saturday church doctrine class just kept me memorizing the rights and wrongs acceptable to God, and how to correct individual failings. As a group, we had a long way to go in our quest for eternal life based on this doctrine, if one believes the doctrine. Again, I had a hard time trying to understand these teachings. It seemed that so many principles of the doctrine were contradictory, when you believed God was Love. I guess even at that time I didn't accept the concept of the Holy Trinity. Why then, I don't know, but it sure was the right decision for me, since I feel more strongly today that God is, God is all there is, there is only God.

Time moved on and by spring of 1947, it became a reality that Harvey had found a new farm to work on shares. Now my father and brother needed to work the two farms. A farm laborer was found and this helped as it took the place of Harvey. I was sure saddened by the fact that my sister and her husband, moved away. The farm they moved to was not that far, but it sure seemed a long way to travel to see them, when they just used to be downstairs.

Now that spring had arrived it was time for me to cram for my graduation from church doctrine class. Palm Sunday was always the time that graduation took place. This was a tradition that started in 1917 and still exists today. The Wednesday before Palm Sunday the class had to be presented to the church congregation. The class sat in chairs in the front of the congregation and was questioned on specific meanings of the church doctrine. Each class member had to answer a question when asked. No one was skipped. All went very well and we graduated. Yeah! Now it was time to think and prepare for the county exams.

With the help of the hired laborer, my father and brother were able to handle the work load. My mother, sisters and I helped all we could. It was a rough summer for all of us not so much from the work, but the idea of Harvey and Doris were working elsewhere, and it felt like something was really missing. I think it was because the family circle had been broken, even if we still got together at special dinners.

Both graduations completed, it was time to think about going to high school in the fall. It was a big year for me completing church doctrine classes and now the eighth grade. I would certainly miss Mrs. Fenelon and her special guidance through some pretty rough times for me. As far as she was concerned, there was her positive statement, "Don't worry Allan you will do just fine. Study hard and as you progress through high school just do the best you can, and that is all that anyone can ask, and that is all I want you to remember". God love her.

A MAJOR CHANGE IN THE FAMILY

Harvey and Doris were working another farm on shares. Phyllis and her husband, Les, were living with his parents. Jerry and Iris were working the Lange second farm. My parents tried to work the homestead, but even with a hired helper it certainly was a struggle. I had just completed the eighth grade and the church doctrine classes, and now I was preparing for high school that began in fall. We all muddled through with the harvesting and other major needed repairs.

I knew my folks found it difficult to keep up with all the tasks that needed to be done. I tried to help as much as I was able. I really only had a general knowledge of what order the work had to be accomplished, so I needed a lot of direction on a daily basis. My parents knew I wanted to help them, but at the same time, I could feel the tension of their burdens. They couldn't afford to hire more laborers and rented as much of the land as they possibly could to the canning company without cutting into food production for the livestock.

At the end of the summer of 1947, and before I started high school, my parents decided to try renting the farm to a younger family. By spring of 1948 a family entered into an agreement with my parents. They would work the farm, but allow us to live in the house, until we could find a place to move.

In August of 1948, my folks purchased a home in nearby Waupun. We moved to the purchased house in the middle of August. This was a big change for me. It meant I no longer had to catch the 6:00am school bus. Also, I would be able to walk to school and go home for lunch. After school, I wouldn't have to ride the bus and arrive home at about 6:00pm. What joy!

Every day my father drove to my brother's place and helped him with the farm work. It was not the same for him, and you could see it in his face. A lot of the old spark he exhibited while working the farm was dying. He, however, began to monitor me more closely and applied more pressure with the career in the ministry idea.

In my first year of high school I had a teacher in algebra by the name of Mrs. Mary Norenberg. She quickly found out that I was proficient in mathematics, and started to challenge my abilities. Once again, I was in a world I understood and enjoyed. Often times she gave me problems to take home for extra credit. I enjoyed the additional work, and unless I blew the exams an "A" was mine.

My other classes were English, History, Health, Biology and Physical Education. During my third year of high school, I took Geometry, Physics and Chemistry. In the chemistry class our church minister's daughter, Rachel, was assigned as my laboratory partner. She depended heavily on me and she admitted her knowledge of chemistry was lacking, I am not sure, but I think she received a "C" for her efforts even with my help.

When my folks learned that Rachel was my lab partner in Chemistry the pressure was on me to ask her out on a date. I wasn't at all interested in her even though she was pretty. A minister's daughter, man, that promised to be a crunch on my opened minded approach to maybe getting involved with the science world. Rachel wasn't the least bit interested in science. What to talk about on a date was a real question. So I told a white lie about her interest in someone else. The folks bought the story and never pressured me again about dating her.

I went to church just about every Sunday and at the insistence of my folks I became an usher and a Sunday school assistant teacher. I guess the church was hard up for teachers. I continued both ushering and teaching the fourth grade Sunday School Class through my high school days.

So life became one of school and church. My after school activities consisted of band and the glee club singing group. Other activities focused on playing softball and shooting pool at a friend's house. This meant that most of my mind was occupied by something other then the problems of my troubled thoughts with church and science philosophies. It was really good to be somewhat free to enjoy the other activities.

So the years moved on and my father and brother got into each others sandbox, so to speak. My father took a job at the local concrete block factory. "It is harder than farm work", he often told my mother.My father continued to work there until a friend convinced him that he should work at the local foundry. The work was just as hard, but the hourly pay was a lot better, and the work hours shorter. This proved to be a win-win situation for my father.

In the summer of 1948 I took a job at the Super Ice Cream Shop at 10 Fond du Lac Street. I could rid my bicycle to work and come home from work for lunch. Mother always had the meal ready and when she wasn't there, peanut butter and jelly sandwiches became a staple meal. Sometimes she would utter a comment and told me to eat other things more healthful. That's when I discovered a wonderful fried egg and catsup sandwich combination. This also brought raised eyebrows, and a reminder, "there are some leftovers in the fridge you just have to heat them up on the stove". No microwave ovens in those days. I would whine and tell her it took too long and I had to get back to school or work depending on the time of year.

In early spring of 1951, I had to apply to the college I expected to attend after high school graduation. It was no contest, Wartburg or work. I took Wartburg along with the idea of at least giving the ministry a try.

Wartburg College is a school associated with the Lutheran Church. It is located in Waverly, Iowa, about 250 miles southwest of Waupun. I decided I would try to please my parents since they were paying for the tuition and books. I worked for extra money during the summer at the local canning company, Canned Foods Inc., for the pea and lima bean harvest. I was the operator of the size grading equipment or as it is called "the pea and bean grader". The last two weeks of August and first week of September I worked for Green Giant Company of Fox Lake, a town five miles to the south of Waupun. I worked there during the night shift boxing canned corn. During the school year, I had a part time job at the college. My Super Ice Cream Shop experience came in handy, as the part time job was at the college snack bar.

I also worked in the college radio station, KWAR 89.9 FM, and soon received a chance to record a program for the major station located in nearby Waterloo, Iowa. The program was liked for its country and western format. I enjoyed the work and for my efforts received an award for outstanding radio broadcasting. Some years later, in 1976, I attended the Don Martin School for Broadcasting in Los Angeles. I received a certificate in Broadcasting and a third class FCC license.

My first college classes consisted of core subjects such as English, History, a science, and two Christianity courses. The two Christianity classes were completely different. One consisted of straight Lutheran doctrine. The second was a free thinking approach to religion. During the class we were asked what we thought religion meant. When I provided input the professor, Dr. Karl Schmidt, gave me a research paper to write and present to the class. The subject was a paper on comparing the major religions of Islam, Hinduism, Judaism, Buddhism and Christianity.

Hours of research and many nights with little sleep were spent reading and trying to find a way to present the paper. I summed up the material and came to the conclusion they all believed in one superior being or entity. This was a very interesting fact. The difference was the approach they took. Well the comments came at me hot and heavy, but in the end I survived and it ended on a happy note for me. I never changed my belief or opinions.

I decided that the ministry was not for me and when I started my third year of college I told my folks of my decision. First my dad just wouldn't hear of it, but my mother defended me and tried to calm him down. He did threaten to stop paying the tuition and gave the "it is the ministry or work, take your choice" ultimatum. But mom convinced him otherwise, so I went back to Wartburg.

During the third year, I got a notice from the draft board of my status change from 4-A to 1-A and my time for the call up was early in 1954. I decided to join the Air Force instead. I told my folks about two weeks before I had to report for duty. I did this to limit the amount of time, I would have to listen to my father rant and rave about it. Mom was saddened but understood my feelings. I explained that I was close to being drafted by the Army in early 1954 and with the enlistment, I would avoid the Army and they would not have to pay the college tuition. I think my mother breathed a sigh of relief on not having to make the payment, and that I would not be a soldier. To her an airman was a safer duty.

I left Wartburg the early part of December 1953 with some regrets, as I knew I would certainly miss the wonderful professors that helped me begin to understand myself.

Off to the Air Force and some really major changes that were about to happen in my life, and it was all for the better. I was more focused and developed a driving ambition to accomplish a dream of finding out what science was all about.

EPILOGUE

Wisdom, information, an idea, is a link between the metaphysical
Creator and the physical creation. It is the hidden face of God.

Gerald L. Schroeder, Author of "THE HIDDEN FACE OF GOD"

After four years in the Air Force, I was discharged from the 1005th Special Investigation Group in Washington, D.C. in October 1957. About a year before my discharge, I met the love of my life, Patricia, and I decided to try to find a job In the D.C. area. The unemployment at the time was about 13 per cent.

I was very lucky and found a laboratory technician position with Atlantic Research located in Alexandria, Virginia. The job involved working with a group on developing rocket propellant. During this time, I worked for Dr. John Nugent, as he was assigned a government project for the development of propellant for the Minute Man Missile. Under his tutelage, I took an extreme interest in the work we were doing, and he encouraged me to study some of the papers he had written. During our many discussions, he approached me with the idea of going back to college. I first considered taking courses at Georgetown University at night, but I would have to repeat some of the courses I had already taken at Wartburg College.

The alternate course was to return to Wartburg College, where I could continue where I left off. My major would be Physics and I could graduate in two and a half years by going full time. God knows when I would have finished, if I attended college only part-time. I followed this course of action and enrolled in Wartburg, starting the second semester that began in January 1958. Patricia and I packed our belongings which all fit (including an ironing board and a big brass plate) in my 1952 Pontiac and drove to Waverly, Iowa.

The trip was filled with memories of snow storms, icy roads and freezing temperatures. When we arrived in Waverly, the sun was very bright and it reflected off the clean white snow.

The temperature was a minus five degrees. At first we thought the temperature indicator on the bank marquee was broken, but we exited the car and knew it had to be correct.

We were married on March 1, 1958, and rented an apartment on the second floor at 1115 First Avenue, N.W. near the college. The house had no insulation and most winter days, we wore heavy sweaters inside. The heating was supplied by a single oil burning stove. Every night I had to go downstairs and fill a five gallon can with fuel oil, then pour it into the tank in the back of the burner. The fuel oil had its odor and it always left an aroma in the apartment after filling. In the spring, the gardens were planted, and we received many vegetables from our landlord and our neighbors. With Patricia working at Schield-Bantam Co. and my GI Bill, plus a part-time job we were able to survive.

I had to study hard, but enjoyed my courses in mathematics, physics and chemistry. I also took American Religions, as an elective. with the same professor I had previously. My assignment was to write a similar paper that I had written, except to intensify the differences between the major religions of America and compare them to those of the world. It was during this time that my belief in God was reinforced, which has grown stronger over the years.

My time at Wartburg passed quickly, and on graduation day, in June of 1960, my mother, father, brother Jerry and sister-in-law Iris drove to Waverly for the graduation ceremony. I could see the pride that my parents had after they saw my degree. Although I knew my father wished that I had pursued a career in the ministry, he was happy for us. He did say he "never thought he would live to see the day". My brother congratulated me as well, although, he was dubious of the value of my degree.

My first job after graduation was an engineering position with Transitron Electronics, in Wakefield, Massachusetts. I was assigned to the transistor and diode production area, and it was my first involvement with the integrated circuit world. It was the beginning of what has exploded into world wide usage for computers and communication electronics.

Following Transitron Electronics, I took a position as an Applied Scientist for the Laboratory for Electronics in Boston, Massachusetts. I worked on bonding techniques to create ultra-high frequency delay lines for radar systems on the Defense Early Warning System.

In 1963 I accepted an offer with General Dynamics of Pomona, California. As a design engineer, I worked on several missile systems built for the United States Military. During my years at General Dynamics, I was assigned to the launch facility at Cape Canaveral, Florida as a flight test engineer for the Atlas Launch Vehicle. The Atlas was used to launch the Agena vehicle, that was the target for the Gemini Space Capsule link-up, as a checkout of the upcoming Apollo missions. The assignment was a thrill of a lifetime for both of us, as we witnessed the beginning of our manned space ventures. Seven months later, I reported back to Pomona to work on critical Viet Nam air strike missiles.

In October of 1972, I accepted a position with Hughes Aircraft Company, Culver City, California. I primarily used my expertise in component and systems testing. I worked on a number of future defense systems and space programs. In the meantime, I received my Master of Science degree in June 1974. In February 1991, as co-inventor, I received a U.S. Patent for "Micro-connector to Micro-strip Controlled Impedance".

In September of 1994 I was awarded the Dr. Malcolm Currie Award for Innovation.

I retired from Hughes Aircraft Co. on November 1, 1994.

And so it was for me a boy born on a farm with dreams he than could not understand, but was able to search out and find the answers to nagging questions between God and science. After those winter nights of lying in the white snow and looking at the clear black sky with the white stars I have found "the hidden face of God" from my career. I truly feel that as we gain in knowledge and wisdom and head to deeper space, that we will be able to reach out and touch the face of God.

After years of study and work, I look back at my accomplishments and I am satisfied. I really enjoyed the journey my career has taken me on, and I was able to witness and become part of real advancements in technology.

Now I can say: "Yes Mrs. Fenelon I did do the very best that I could".

APPENDICIES

APPENDIX 1

Harvey and The Queen Mary

Harvey returned from the Philippines aboard the Queen Mary. The ship was used as a troop carrier during WWII.

In 1978, Harvey and Doris came to visit Patricia and I in the Silver Lake District of Los Angeles, California. During their visit he mentioned the fact that he had returned from the war on the Queen Mary. He wanted to know if it was close to where we lived, and if it was possible to go see the ship in Long Beach. We certainly were happy to take them to see it.

During our self-guided tour of the ship, he gave us a description of how the troops were packed into the ship. There were beds set up in the drained swimming pool on the upper deck, where the soldiers slept. He took us to the ball room where the movies were often shown. He recounted the thirty day journey of the trip, and many times he drifted to those days, and it told a story of its own in his face. It left a lasting impression on Patricia and I.

APPENDIX 2

LADOGA

Ladoga or "Dog Town" as it is affectionately referred to, is a place of significant history. It is located at the intersection of highways 26 and 103 (now TC). It was once a stagecoach stop for people traveling from Green Bay to Milwaukee in about the year 1846. The original tavern located at the southwest corner of the highway intersection was called The Rising Sun Tavern run by a Mr. Whalex. The first general store which also housed the post office was run by Ray Wilkinson for 48 years. Later businesses included a harness and shoe repair, and a butter factory. A later addition to the area was a car agency owned by Lyle Brown. Lyle later sold the agency to Ren Miller. Ren later expanded it to include tractors and other farm machinery. He also added the gasoline station and garage facilities. A feed mill was built a few years later providing a big help to the local farmers.

A brief history of Ladoga and the inhabitants is summarized very well in the Waupun Leader News of October 27, 1976. A book is being written about Ladoga but the publication date is not known.

APPENDIX 3

Mother's Dresses

A lot of the dresses my mother and sisters wore were hand sewn by my mother and sister Doris. They would buy material and patterns for the dress from the local fabric store. My younger sister, Phyllis, worked with both of them and later sewed dresses herself.

The war years created a shortage of fabric at the store and for some reason the feed manufacturers started to package the feed into very colorful fabric, which became a source for the women of the household for their dresses. Some patterns on the bag material fit into the fashion of the time. Almost every woman made dresses or blouses from the bag material, which I remember as being a heavier cotton. The fabric lasted through many washings even to the point where the design had faded away.

I remember that when my father went to buy feed mother would go along and frustrate him by having to look through all the bags for the fabric material she wanted. There was also a problem, if not enough material of one printed fabric was available, a new design would have to be considered. This certainly slowed down the purchase time, until she made up her mind. Dad was about to bounce off the wall, but kept quiet about it.

Fortunately I never received a shirt of "many colors".

APPENDIX 4

THE FARM HOUSE

The house that I was born in was built by my grandfather, father and two uncles. It was a wood three story frame construction with a basement. The first floor contained the entryway, kitchen, dining room, living room and two bedrooms. One bedroom was my parents and the other was my grandparent's bedroom. The second story housed five bedrooms, where my sisters and I slept, my room being the smallest. Two of the remaining bedrooms were designated as the guest bedrooms. The basement had a couple of rooms with shelves that held the canned goods and root vegetables. The basement had no furnace. It had a cistern that was used to store rainwater. When it rained the water ran into the cistern by a pipe attached to the gutters that ran along the roof.

The foundation was the most interesting part of the whole building. The basement was dug using a large scoop that was pulled by two horses. Two men handled the scoop handles. It was set upright on the ground and as the horses move forward the scoop dug its way into the ground and was levered upward until the scoop was full and dragged to an area and dumped. This continued until the basement area was cleared. The sides of the dirt were scraped vertically with shovels. Once the basement area was ready the many large stones gathered from the farm fields were put into place and filled with a mortar made from ground stone, sand and a binder of some nature. Once the basement and foundation were finished the house was then constructed.

I would estimate the building contained about 5500 square feet. This included an attic which served as dead air space for insulation, storage and during the summer a play area for me, when it rained outside. During the winter it served as a cool place to store food.

MY PARENTS

EDWARD LUDWIG LANGE
dob: April 18, 1893 bpl. Brandon, WI
dod: May 2, 1976
    son/of AUGUST Wilhelm Lange
    dob: June 18, 1853 bpl: Treptow-Toll, Germany
    dod: February 8, 1944 dpl: Waupun, Wisconsin
    md. October 7, 1882 mpl: Germany
    m.. OTTILIA Berger
    dob: November 8, 1860 bpl: Germany
    dod: January 30, 1934 dpl: Waupun, Wisconsin
md. August 26, 1914
m. ESTHER WILEMINIA BERTHA BORCHARDT
dob May 13, 1895 bpl: Montpelier, Wisconsin
dod: August 16, 1983
    dau/of HERMAN F. Borchardt
    dob: November 18, 1845, bpl: Pommern, Germany
    dod: November 17, 1920 dpl: Rosendale, Wisconsin
    md. November 8, 1873, mpl. Wisconsin
    m. AMELIA Thurow
    dob: December 13, 1854 bpl. Pommern, Germany
    dod: December 5, 1929
son: Gerald John Charles m. Iris Thalacker
    children: Carolyn May; Betsy Lee, Orlin Glen
dau: Doris Mildred m. Harvey Rahn
    son: Darrell Edward
dau: Phyllis Mae 1st m. Leslie Zuege
    sons: Wayne Edward; Dale Leslie; Lee Arthur; Russell Charles
    2nd m. Lawrence Harder
    son: Todd Bryan
son: Allan Edward
    m. Patricia Reid

Doris and Darrell, Phyllis and Wayne

Phyllis in Formal

Orlin, Betsy and Farmal Tractor

Grandmother and Grandfather
(Ottilia and August Lange Sr.)

A story is just a story, a life is just a life
but a story about a way of life is a treasure
that can only be realized, if it is recorded
for others to read.

Father and Mother (Edward and Esther Lange)